DORSET VOL I

Edited by Carl Golder

GW00702030

First published in Great Britain in 1999 by
POETRY NOW YOUNG WRITERS
1-2 Wainman Road, Woodston,
Peterborough, PE2 7BU
Telephone (01733) 230748

HB ISBN 0 75430 253 9
SB ISBN 0 75430 254 7

FOREWORD

With over 63,000 entries for this year's Cosmic competition, it has proved to be our most demanding editing year to date.

We were, however, helped immensely by the fantastic standard of entries we received, and, on behalf of the Young Writers team, thank you.

Cosmic Dorset Vol I is a tremendous reflection on the writing abilities of 8 & 9 year old children, and the teachers who have encouraged them must take a great deal of credit.

We hope that you enjoy reading *Cosmic Dorset Vol I* and that you are impressed with the variety of poems and style with which they are written, giving an insight into the minds of young children and what they think about the world today.

CONTENTS

Haymoor Middle School

Anna Saunders	13
Kay Bunter	13
Rachel Hunt	14

Hill View Primary School

Dean Northeast	14
Alice Keeping	15
Kayleigh Oliver	15
Nathan Rawlings	16
William Dao	16
Steven James Lane	17
Louis Walter	17
Sophie Power	18
Gary Vinton	18
Daniel Thompson	19
Hannah Prentice	19
Lisa Barnes	20
Abbey Squibb	20
Emily Knight	21
Hannah Cowdrill	22
Hannah Kimber	22
Jamie Matthew Wills	23
Verity Cutler	23
Kimberley Rowland	24
Matthew Jones	24
Christopher Smith	24
Alex Holgate	25
Samantha Kerley	25
Marcus Hagg	25
Jamie Thomson	26
Michelle Cummings	26
Amy Cox	27
Matthew Clarke	27
Joe Gilbey	28

Megan Harling	60
Megan Baker	60
Emma Balderstone	61
Daniel Benham	61
Jessica Fletcher	61
Carla Miles	62

Milldown Middle School

Kate Kellaway-Moore	62
Kim Fendley	63
Simon Hayter	63
Sarah Morris	64
Ben Wentworth	64
Rebecca Whalley	65
Gavin Kerby	65
Charlotte Adams	66
Anthony Woodruff	66
Rebecca Hunterwood	67
Philip Martin	68
Tanya Pentney	68
Naomi Kendrick	69
Glen Wareham	69
Stacey White	70
Luke Mason	70
Holly Morrison	71
Christopher Wareham	71
Lisa Plested	72
Thomas Hill	72
Tara Cheese	73
Candice Asher	73
Jessica Toledo	74

Radipole CP School

Eleanor Hunt & Briony Warren	74
Hannah Gibson	75
Amelia Williams	75

St Mary's School, Beaminster

Shirley Dorran	76
Natalie Stewart	76
Michael Livens	76
Nick Hill	77
Tia Corry Wright	77
Laura Crabb	78
Lydia Olsen	78

St Nicholas & St Lawrence School

Hannah Clark	79

St Thomas Garnet's Primary School

Robert West	79
Sean Dingley	80
Rebecca Green	80
Anne Henman	81
Ben Hitchcock	81
Elizabeth McMahon	82
Kae Drinkwater	82
James Ingram-Johnson	83
Lee Fordham	83
Christopher Linda	84
Sean Atkinson	84
Christopher Short	85
Theresa Gillings	85
Paul Malin	86
Anna Wazejewski	86
Emma Tuck	87
Gareth Wilson	88

Alexander Simmons	89
Fionnuala Craven	90
Oisin O'Leary	90
Bethany Wildeman	90
Anya Browne	91
Grace Watt	92
Laura Sheasby	93

Sherborne Preparatory School

James Massson	94
Sonja Farrell	94
Simon Horner	95
Mark Corfield-Moore	96
Jamie Smibert	96
Sophie Weller	97
Lucy Crocker	98
Robert Smith	98
Jonathan Hacking	99
Lucinda James	100
Ratidzo Moyo	100
Jackie Cameron	101

Sticklands VA Primary School

Lucy Mather	101
Molly Davies-Crosby	102
Jody Mason	102
Edmond Wright	103
Joanne O'Donovan	104
Leanne Knight	104
Ellie Chapman	105
Ashley Jones	105

THE POEMS

COSMIC

Up here on the moon
Counting the holes.
Craters huge, spaces, valleys.
Deep, deep pits, moon creatures.
Mountains with strange trees are everywhere.
Lots of stars sparkling up high.
Twinkling balls of fiery gas for showing their light.
Millions of miles.

Cara Turner (9)
All Saints Primary School

COSMIC

C razy creatures on Mars.
O n the moon there are big holes.
S aturn way out in space.
M ars is a planet in space.
I   ce is nearly everywhere on Pluto.
C raters in space, floating around in fine air.

James Axe (9)
All Saints Primary School

COSMIC

Looking down on land and sea,
With white clouds all around.
What a lovely scene it is to see from above,
So come on up and have a look to see
What I can see.

Lucy Parsons (9)
All Saints Primary School

COSMIC

Stars up in the sky
Sparkling and twinkling.
Little flashes of lights,
Inky-black sky
Crescent-shaped moon.
Pale-yellow shining in the inky-black sky.
Dark craters holding secrets,
Will life be found in them?

Toby Frost (9)
All Saints Primary School

COSMIC

Crazy creatures out in Mars.
Shaped all different, like a monster's face.
Icy mountains melting now.
Poor old Mars is getting weak.

Mars is fading, fading away.
Now we'll have to say goodbye
To poor old Mars.

Natasha Dodge (9)
All Saints Primary School

COSMIC

Clouds darken, block out the sunlight,
That shines from the moon.
Shining stars far out in space.
Mars spinning near -
Can I see crazy creatures?

Brady Harcom (9)
All Saints Primary School

COSMIC

Calm and peaceful earth,
Green and blue - land and sea,
Spinning, turning on its axis,
Sun in the south because it is noon,
Icy white clouds lurk over the earth,

Out in icy darkness,
Planets spin, like the earth,
But they hold no water - and therefore
    no life
Earth is unique
... you'll never find one like it.

Verity Cuff (9)
All Saints Primary School

COSMIC

Looking down from the moon
Strange creatures all around
It is very silent and calm
Swirling clouds cover mountains
Strange trees everywhere.

Dust settles on my boots
Just in the distance Mars and Pluto
Huge creatures surround me.

Emma Fairclough (9)
All Saints Primary School

PLANET COSMIC

On a planet far away.
Cosmic people go to play.
The cosmic horses are eating hay.
Everyone is happy today.
Because it is cosmic day in May.
We are going back today.
10, 9, 8, 7, 6, 5, 4, 3, 2, 1 *go!*
I think my heart will start to flow.
Oh no! Here we go, we're losing petrol.
Zooming home into the middle of a dome.
Boo! Now I will have to walk home.

Hannah Terry (8)
Bransgore Primary School

WINNING TENNIS

I've got my racket,
I'm ready to serve,
The ball is flying,
Round the curve,
It touches the ground,
And bounces away,
To win there is a way,
I feel so excited,
I have won,
I'm so delighted,
I knew I could win,
I'm the tennis king.

Katie Dancey (8)
Bransgore Primary School

IN SPACE

When I went into space.
I saw a slimy alien with a big pace,
But when I saw his ugly face,
I turned around to the stars,
Then I landed on Mars,
The planet was very red,
Just then I tripped and bumped my head
I went inside my spaceship it usually goes bop,
It has springs on the top,
And rings on the side,
The alien's coming it's time to hide,
Now I think it's time to land,
I landed on some very soft sand.

Philip Worden (8)
Bransgore Primary School

MOON

The moon is big
The moon is round
I go up in a rocket
10, 9, 8, 7, 6, 5, hope I stay alive
4, 3, 2, 1, 0, lift-off!
I see the moon above me
I see aliens pink and brown
They're so big, they make me frown
It was cold, the aliens were bold
It was very bumpy and jumpy
I eat so quick, I'm going to be sick
I've got to get down.

Michael Garlick (8)
Bransgore Primary School

DO YOU KNOW ME?

I live in the sea
Around new Zealand.
Come and see me,
I swim near the sand.

I play with my friends,
They call it a pod.
We do leaps and bends,
Together we nod.

My skin's soft and smooth,
And two colours of grey.
I splash when I move,
And have babies in May.

I have fishes for tea,
I swim with my fins.
Come play with me,
I'm a dusky dolphin.

Joanna Pennington (8)
Bransgore Primary School

MY BROTHER

My brother is a disgrace,
He pulls my hair, he scratches my face
He rolls on his back, he is six months old.
All he wants to do is be bold.
He likes to play all day long.
You would think he is weak
But he is very strong!

Leanda Westall (8)
Bransgore Primary School

6

IN SPACE

We are taking-off 10, 9, 8, 7, 6, 5, 4, 3, 2, 1, *go!*
We are in the rocket, start to flow
Go fast no, no it's not a race
I think I've got a red face
We are here, jump out
Have you got a little spout?
It's scary out here
But the lights are on at Bournemouth pier
It's dark
Look, some aliens are playing in the park
It's really bumpy
Stop being miserable and grumpy
It is cold and freezing
Stop sneezing
But it is dusty
And blustery.

Natalie King (8)
Bransgore Primary School

MY PET DOG

One day out walking with my dog.
He suddenly made friends with a hog.
I tried and I tried but he wouldn't come back.
But when he did he was dressed-up in black.
I cleaned all the paw prints all over the house.
While he was chasing a cute and furry mouse.

Tarryn Troye (9)
Bransgore Primary School

TWILIGHT NIGHT

At the strike of twilight,
It is very plain to see it is twilight night,
The stars shine bright,
And the moon is at its height,
Other people call it twilight might.

Sometimes we call it the twilight fright,
But it is nothing to do with twilight zone,
And nothing to do with 'ET phone home',
It is just twilight,
When the stars shine beautiful,
And bright.

Jordan Newport (9)
Bransgore Primary School

WONDERFUL PONIES

Prancing, dancing ponies, jumping,
Obstinate, stubborn ponies, stopping,
Naughty, nibbling ponies, biting,
Intelligent, brainy ponies, thinking,
Energetic, frisky ponies, galloping,
Special, precious ponies to treasure.

Emma Rodell (8)
Bransgore Primary School

TREES

The trees have lots of leaves,
Then the dogs come along with fleas.
The bark is the colour brown and has a little frown.

Georgie Corsby (8)
Bransgore Primary School

IMAGINARY SPACE

Ready to launch . . . boom!
We're lifting up high,
This is great!
Bye, bye,
My rocket is blue with yellow spots,
With orange springs,
And as I hear,
They all go ping,
Now I see Mars,
The planet so red,
Did I just see,
Super Ted?
There's an alien,
So gruesome I see,
He's got green dots,
Right on his knee,
Time to land,
On a different planet,
Doesn't it look,
Like Titanic?
This surface so rough,
The land so dry,
Now I know,
What makes me fly,
Back up I go,
To earth down low,
Now there's an alien,
Oh no!

Brett Joy (8)
Bransgore Primary School

PLAYING SNOOKER

To play snooker you need a cue,
Remember to make sure it's the size for you.
Potting the reds is quite hard,
Sometimes you only have to step a yard.
On the table you have a cloth,
But it's not the colour of a moth.
In snooker there are lots of balls,
Some of them are as hard as walls.
Winning the championship is really brill,
Some day you really will.

Michael Pope (8)
Bransgore Primary School

WHY?

Why does this happen?
People dying
everywhere in the world.
Look what's happening
God's creation
Look! Open your eyes.
Famine and disaster
Pollution
creatures dying every day.
Look right now!
Stop and think!
What can you do?
How can I help
the human race
and everything living today?

Rebekah Crease (9)
Christ The King Primary School

WAITING

I dread being sick,
I hate going shopping with my mum,
I hate school,
I hate going to the doctors,
I hate my sister shouting,
I hate Mum shouting.

I am over the top when people come over to sea,
When it is Christmas too,
When it is my birthday,
I'm excited,
I am happy when I am swimming.

Paul Crane (9)
Gillingham Milton CE School

AUTUMN

Blackberries, blackberries juicy and black,
Gather them, gather them in a big sack.
Clematis, clematis climbing up high,
The white bryony nearby.
White bryony, white bryony shiny and red,
In a cosy snug bed.

Holly Toomer (9)
Gillingham Milton CE School

THE OWL

As he leaves his branch,
He spreads his wings out wide,
Looking like a large moth in the darkness,
His brightly coloured golden-yellow eyes,
Are like headlights on a car,
As he glides silently through the night.
He swoops down,
When he spots his prey,
He snatches it up,
With his sharp claws,
And devours it in one gulp.

Oliver Hibbs (9)
Gillingham Milton CE School

MY WINTER POEM

I go outside I feel the cold
I say I better get a coat.
My fingers are numb
My toes are shivering
My nose is as red as a raspberry.
I hope I get a warm dinner today
The mist is flowing out my mouth
Now the snowflakes are blowing in my face.

Rebecca Thomas (9)
Gillingham Milton CE School

A WINTER'S DAY

Can this be day?
It looks like night
So thin and sulky is the light

A lonely sweeper in the street
Disturbs the dust of last night's feet

And singing, singing in my head
How safe it was
How warm in bed.

Anna Saunders (9)
Haymoor Middle School

YELLOW

Yellow is the sun that keeps us warm.
Yellow is the buttercups on the hillside.
Yellow is the daffodils in the valley below.
Yellow is the sour lemon juice on our pancakes.
Yellow is the moon that lights up the sky.
Yellow is the bananas that we and monkeys eat.
Yellow is the sand on the beach we make sandcastles out of.
Yellow is the greatest colour of them *all*.

Kay Bunter (9)
Haymoor Middle School

JONATHAN JOHN

There was a miller,
Who lived by a river,
And his name was Jonathan John,
He tripped over his bucket,
And decided to chuck it,
And went for swim in a pond.

Rachel Hunt (9)
Haymoor Middle School

SPACE - WHAT IS OUT THERE?

Space
is
very
starry.
Filled
with
planets and comets
and shooting
stars and rockets
flying high.

Dean Northeast (9)
Hill View Primary School

THE NIGHT TRAIN

Signal's changed it's time to go,
Children and adults have far to go.
Over the hills and over the plains.
Here it comes, the night train.

Coming slowly to a grinding halt.
Taking with it a gentle jolt.

There goes the Bush family.
The Glows, the Browns.

The guard blows his whistle.
And waves his flag.
There goes the night train.
Into town.

Alice Keeping (8)
Hill View Primary School

OUR EARTH

Our earth is good
Up in space.
Round and round we go.

Earth is round
and it's green and blue.
Round the sun it goes.
The earth is one of the nine planets.
It has lots of people on it.

Kayleigh Oliver (9)
Hill View Primary School

THE HAUNTED HOUSE

We live in a haunted house,
Then we saw a deadly mouse,

Then I saw a glimpse of white,
Then I started to show my fright,

When I made friends with the ghosts,
I made a little ghost,

When I said 'Give me five,'
A deadly mummy just came alive,

One of the ghosts went to fly,
I said. 'Goodbye.'

Nathan Rawlings (9)
Hill View Primary School

STARS

Stars, star so bright
In the air in the night
It glows the dark night
Stars glow like the bright sun.
The stars glow the dark
As the day, as day falls
The stars come zooming out
When night falls stars fade
Away and that is the end
　　　Of the stars.

William Dao (9)
Hill View Primary School

FISH

Fish are fat.
Fish are thin.
So why don't we
teach them to swim?
Bass are stupid.
Bass are clever.
So why do they have
skins of leather?
Lings are dumb.
Lings are fun.
So why do they
try to eat my thumb?
Dab are hard.
Dab are soft.
So why don't they
feel like cloth?

Steven James Lane (8)
Hill View Primary School

ALIENS

Aliens are there, aliens are here
Aliens are from far and near
They come from stars, maybe Mars

They're mean, certainly not clean
One wears smelly wellies
The other has an eye on his belly.

Louis Walter (9)
Hill View Primary School

DOLPHINS

Dolphins splashing in the sun
     Dolphins jumping really high
All they want is a peaceful life
     Sweet, beautiful and cuddly
Their underwater homes are sweet,
     Don't misjudge them for horrible creatures
Sailors laugh when they see them jump up high
     Zoos aren't their natural habitat
They're not cruel but you are
     They miss their family
They're not made for performing on stage.

Sophie Power (8)
Hill View Primary School

THE SILLY GHOST

I saw a ghost eating toast,
Half-way up the chimney.
He fell down,
With his golden crown.
And his spine came tumbling after.
All his friends found it funny.
To see a ghost with no tummy.
So the ghost got a gun.
And shot them all for fun.

Gary Vinton (8)
Hill View Primary School

A HAUNTED HOUSE!

A haunted house!
Spooky
Scary
Monsters
Hairy!

Loud
Lightning
Very
Frightening!

Ghosts and
Ghouls
Playing
Pool!

Lots of
Slime
Where we
Dine!

Vampire
Bats
Kicking
Cats!

Chopped
Off heads
In the
Beds!

Daniel Thompson (8)
Hill View Primary School

MY DOG

My dog Tod is a Yorkshire terrier
He likes to play but he doesn't like the postman,
Every week we give him a bath
Then he rolls in the mud.
Some mornings I take him for a walk
          down and up
                    up and down
          down and up
                    up and down.

Hannah Prentice (9)
Hill View Primary School

IN SPRING

In spring
baby animals
are born
and new plants
are planted.
A new calf
arrives.
A new foal
appears.
A new pig grows
A new
kitten is emerging.
A new puppy
develops.

Lisa Barnes (8)
Hill View Primary School

BONFIRES

Flames in the sky
Not so high
Burning hot
Wood and twig crackling away
Flames flickering everywhere
Pretty colours in the sky
Very, very high
Everyone round the fire
Smoke going higher in the sky

Abbey Squibb (9)
Hill View Primary School

DISNEYLAND PARIS

Disneyland
is an
exciting place lots
of rides, lots
of people to
meet
and even
different lands. Best
of all is Phantom
Manor
lots of
ghosts even ghostly
pianos
playing by
themselves.
Ghosts even
come
up behind
you and
scare you.
Aaaah! Enough
excitement for one
day.
Goodbye Disneyland
Boo, hoo, hoo.
It's
a very
pleasant sight to
see.

Emily Knight (9)
Hill View Primary School

CATS

C ats are fat
A lso thin
T hey are fluffy
S ome bald

C ats are black
A lso white
T hey are ginger
S ome grey

C ats are good
A lso bad
T hey are soft
S ome rough

C ats eat mice
A lso birds
T hey eat fish
S ome Whiskas

C ats live on farms
A lso streets
T hey live in houses
S ome in shops

Hannah Cowdrill (8)
Hill View Primary School

RABBITS

Twitchy noses wriggle all the day.
Nibbling white teeth chewing on hay.
Furry strong legs gently hopping.
Warmly floppy.

Hannah Kimber (8)
Hill View Primary School

ALIENS

Aliens are spooky
and have a weird transport.
I don't think you'd ever catch
them playing any sport.
Aliens are not science fiction.
They are not a form of addiction.
Aliens are brown and wrinkly things
And if they walked past a shop then
the alarm would ring.
Aliens don't have names but at some point
they go insane.
If lightning's striking then there is going to be
an alien sighting.

Jamie Matthew Wills (8)
Hill View Primary School

MY CAT

My cat's golden-brown
Streaks of orange
Flashes of white

She's called Fudge
She gets up to mischief
In the night

She grabs your hands
Playing about
Sleeping most of the time
That's my cat Fudge.

Verity Cutler (9)
Hill View Primary School

FLOWERS

Pretty flowers
Colourful flowers
Summer flowers
Winter flowers
Autumn flowers
Spring flowers
Perfumed flowers
That's what I call flowers.

Kimberley Rowland (9)
Hill View Primary School

SPRING

S mell the beautiful
P lants are growing
R abbits hopping around.
I insects in the soil.
N ice white clouds.
G reat acorn trees.

Matthew Jones (8)
Hill View Primary School

SPRING

S pring is green and red colours.
P eople are enjoying themselves in the spring.
R ipening trees everywhere.
I slands of green and orange.
N uts being eaten by squirrels.
G reen grass everywhere.

Christopher Smith (8)
Hill View Primary School

VAMPIRES

Red bloodthirsty vampires
In the moonlight
Licking their teeth
Red eyes like blood
Steaming in on their prey
Steaming yummy blood
Their hunger is no more.

Alex Holgate (8)
Hill View Primary School

SPRING

S quirrels so you can hear them digging.
P ink tulips flowering.
R abbits hopping excitedly everywhere.
I nteresting deer running at night.
N ight owls passing.
G reen bushy grass swaying.

Samantha Kerley (8)
Hill View Primary School

SPRING

S pring has colour.
P ink roses smell.
R ed tomatoes grow on fruit trees
I nsects can fly.
N uts for squirrels.
G rass is green.

Marcus Hagg (7)
Hill View Primary School

SPRING POEM

S ounds from the spring birds
  Oh how lovely the birds can sing.
P urple brightens my house, purple brightens my street
  Oh how lovely, I love purple
R ed is a feeling of summer, red is feeling of my heart
  Oh I do love the smell of flowers
I love the smell of spring
  I love the smell of everything including you and me.
N ice is spring, nice is my heart
  Nice is including you and me.
G reen is a very bright colour.
  I'd say brighter than you and me.

Jamie Thomson (8)
Hill View Primary School

SPRING POEM

S pring comes when the blossom turns to
  its normal pink colour.
P urple flowers smelling sweet.
R oses are red.
I like the sound of the ants crawling along
  the path munching their food.
N ow it's spring, the birds are getting ready
  it's spring.
G athering at the trees, spring, spring, spring.

Michelle Cummings (8)
Hill View Primary School

HURRICANE

At first it was very plain
But then I saw a *hurricane!*
A whirlwind was there (like company)
And they were heading straight for *me!*
I saw them coming. I started to yelp!
'Help me! Help me! Help! Help! Help!'
It won't just destroy little me,
It will wreck my house and family
I did not know what to say
'Cos the hurricane blew away!
And then it started to rain
And never a hurricane came again.

Amy Cox (8)
Hill View Primary School

SUMMERTIME

The sun is shining in the sky,
The birds are singing in the trees,
Children playing beside the sea,
I really like the summertime.

The buzzing bees inside the flowers,
Getting the pollen to make the honey,
Ice-lollies melting in the sun,
I really like the summertime.

Matthew Clarke (9)
Hill View Primary School

HALLOWE'EN IS A SCREAM

Yes it's Hallowe'en,
Time to give yourself a scream
Oh, look here comes the skeleton football team,
Just watch their bones shimmer and gleam.
In a very dark creepy house,
Inside there's not even a mouse.
Well, apart from a slimy green ghoul,
That haunts you when you walk down the hall.
Inside a shut down school,
You can hear witches' voices shout and bawl.
'Yawn, oh look, it's nearly morning,'
'Yawn I just can't stop yawning.'
By the time you've settled down in bed,
Before you know it, you're dead.

Joe Gilbey (9)
Hill View Primary School

LITTLE CAT

Little cat sat in a chair
Getting up to go somewhere.

Saw a mouse
Down the side of the house.

Chased it all
Round and round.

Joanne Scammell (8)
Hill View Primary School

Spring Poem

S pring is colourful.
P eeping blossom in the breeze.
R abbits jumping round the trees.
I n spring the blossom comes out.
N uts falling off the trees.
G leaming leaves coming back on the trees.
S pring is delightful.

Peter Scott (8)
Hill View Primary School

Rabbit Poem

Jumping, hopping
Around the garden
Sometimes stopping to eat
The grass
Barney.

Jessica Hailes (7)
Hill View Primary School

Spring

S pring is a nice green colour
P lants and flowers are growing
R ain is shining in the sun
I nsects wriggling in the dirt
N ice blue sky, nice white clouds
G ardens as beautiful as rain.

Hannah Moore (7)
Hill View Primary School

Spring Poem

S pring is on its way.
P lants are growing.
R abbits are popping out of their burrows.
I n the garden children play.
N ightingales singing night and day.
G reen leaves are opening
S pring is wonderful.

Sam Cummings (7)
Hill View Primary School

Spring

S unshine's brighter than ever
P retty flowers blossoming
R ivers flowing
I nteresting burrows curling
N ature spreads around us
G etting more beautiful than ever.

James Wallace-Walton (8)
Hill View Primary School

Spring

S pring is coming on its way.
P urple pansies smelling all sweet.
R oses are red.
I like the creepy crawly ants.
N ear the softly flowing river.
G reen grass swaying with the wind.

Tania Gepheart (7)
Hill View Primary School

SPRING POEM

S inging birds tweet, tweet!
P eople have different picnics to eat
R abbits hopping in the fields
I n the fields horses are galloping
N o snow is here
G reen grass is growing instead
S pring is lovely.

Lauren Mountford (8)
Hill View Primary School

SPRING

S pring is a lovely colour.
P lanting lovely flowers.
R ound every tree.
I nsects in the soil.
N ice blue sky.
G rey clouds.

Spring is very, very beautiful.

Oliver Sutcliffe (7)
Hill View Primary School

SPRING

S pring is for lovely flowers.
P is for purple flowers.
R is for red roses.
I nsects - they wriggle in the dirt.
N oisy birds in the trees singing songs.
G rass swaying in the air.

Rebecca Hares (8)
Hill View Primary School

YOUNG PUPPY

Playing and prodding the air,
Pouncing, bouncing here and there.
He jumps upon a butterfly,
A ball of fluff in the sky.

The strong paws, chubby face,
He wants to join the butterfly race.
His wagging tail, little yaps,
Racing round 100 laps.

Oh no, oh no, it got away,
I haven't time now to play.
I think I'd better go in,
But first I'll rummage in the rubbish bin.

Joanna Dey (9)
Hill View Primary School

GHOSTLY GHOULS

Some people say ghostly ghouls are lazy and crazy,
Even clowns' gowns,
Teacher splatted on the wall
By a green kind of ghoul
Just after school in the hall.
Towns and clowns in dressing gowns
Yell 'Aaah, there's a hideous monster'.
After they felt a bit dizzy and fizzy
Ghostly music, horrified faces,
Something frying, people dying.

Enzo Cuglietta (9)
Hill View Primary School

LITTLE LAMB

As I watch him,
Prancing, dancing,
Being cheeky.

While I watch him,
Leaping, sleeping,
Being mischievous.

As I watch him.
Bounding, pounding,
Being sweet.

While I watch him,
Teasing, sneezing,
Being lovely.

As I stroke him,
Bleating, eating,
Being cute.

While I watch him,
Sleeping, snoring,
Fast asleep.

Sophie Herrmann (9)
Hill View Primary School

SPRING

S pring has colourful green shiny leaves.
P opping up, flowers that twinkle all day.
R ippling rivers that feel as clean as air.
I nsects that smell around for food.
N ight comes and all nature goes to sleep.
G arden birds glide about in the shining sun.

Tom Lands (7)
Hill View Primary School

TREES AND LEAVES

Crispy leaves
lovely trees
leaves fluttering
in the breeze.

Active leaves
in the trees
bombastic trees
waving in the breeze.

Curly leaves
stuck to the trees
leaves break off
in the breeze.

Neil James Turle (9)
Hill View Primary School

EASTER

Easter holiday,
Easter eggs,
Happy faces,
Time for bed.

Easter bunny,
Hopping around,
Found a place,
To put them down.
Cool, I've found them
Yum, yum, yum!

Adam Trimby (8)
Hill View Primary School

A WELL DESERVED SNACK

A penguin is a very caring father
He cares for the egg while mum's at sea.
She may be away for up to forty days
But the fish she catches are for herself to eat.

It would be the end for an embryo
If the egg were to touch the snow
So dad has to sit still with the egg on his feet
And dream of fish, fresh from the sea.

Baby penguins are brown and fluffy
They huddle together in a pack.
Meanwhile their parents are away at sea
And their fathers are having a well deserved snack.

Julia Callow (9)
Hill View Primary School

SNOW

The glistening, glittering snow,
soft and gentle snowmen,
freezing, frosty, icy breeze,
blowing through your hair.

Your fingers go numb,
your nose goes bright red,
hands warm with mittens on.

The snow's surface is white and smooth,
trees wear dresses that are
lacy and fine!
Glistening glittering snow.

Rebecca Mason (8)
Hill View Primary School

THE ALIEN WORLD

Alien fish,
Frightening eyes,
Help me!

Horrifying,
Terrifying,
Razor teeth,
Ahh!
It's a shark!

Angel fish,
Lion fish,
Help me!

Now with
All these
Monsters
In the sea
I'm not swimming, not me!

Rebekah Heys (8)
Hill View Primary School

SPRING

S pring has beautiful colours.
P ink tulips have nice smells.
R oses are starting to bud.
I can hear birds singing.
N ature is beautiful.
G reen grass is starting to grow.

Daniel Wilding (8)
Hill View Primary School

IF I WAS AN ALIEN

If I was an alien
I would have a blue tummy
Green googly eyes
Purple legs
And a white face.

If I was an alien
I would eat
Space spaghetti
Galactic chocolate
And pizzas from Pluto.

If I was an alien
I would
Run around backwards
I would have a spaceship
I would drive it backwards
And then round and round.

Fiona Harris (9)
Hill View Primary School

ON MY BIRTHDAY

On Saturday
It was my birthday
I had a party
My friends came round
To my house
I got £50
For my birthday.

Zoe Treadwell (9)
Hill View Primary School

EASTER TIME

Baby chicks hatching
little deer run
bunnies are hopping.
It must be Eastertime.

Growing colourful tulips
tiny little daffodils
short grass growing.
Sunny days are coming.

Sparkling children
happy faces
joyful sunshine.
Spring is arriving.

Little mellow showers
It's Easter.

Karly Hudson (8)
Hill View Primary School

GOING TO HOLIDAY

I'm going on holiday to Spain
Today
Hip hip hooray
I'm going
You can come too
I hope we get brown
Brown yes, that is a holiday.

Violet Francis (9)
Hill View Primary School

I'M A BALLOON

I'm a balloon,
Flying up to the sky.
I'm a balloon,
I'm up very high.
I'm a balloon,
Floating into space.
I'm a balloon,
In an alien race.
I'm a balloon,
That's seen the moon.
I'm a balloon,
That's played an alien bassoon.
I'm a balloon,
That's seen an alien birth.
I'm a balloon,
Descending to earth.
I'm a balloon,
That's died in Devon.
I'm a balloon,
That's gone to heaven.

Elizabeth Manly (9)
Hill View Primary School

SPORT

Sport, sport, I love sport,
Professional like Sheringham,
Over the net, what a mess,
Red card off the pitch, oh no,
Time up, whistle blown.

Ross Mercer (8)
Hill View Primary School

FLOWERS BLOOMING

Flowers blooming brightly
Upon the flower-beds
Poppies, tulips, daffodils
Swaying from side to side
Then I touch a tulip
It is soft and dainty
Flowers look so beautiful, attractive and lovely
Colours crimson, violet and blue
Flowers paraded all over the park
I am so delighted
How I would love to be keeper of the flowers.

Lynda Walker (9)
Hill View Primary School

ICE

Ice is as smooth as glass.
As smooth as smooth as glass.
It's frozen so that
We can skate
Ice is smooth as glass.

Ice is smooth as glass,
As smooth as smooth as glass.
Shivering penguins skate on the ice
The ice which is as smooth as glass
As smooth as smooth as glass.

Benjamin Lewis (8)
Hill View Primary School

THE EASTER BUNNY

'Night Mum'
The lights are out
But who's that creeping through
He's coming to the window
Now he's in,
A basket in his right hand.
He's pulling something out
Hey, it's an egg!
No, it's an Easter egg.
One on top of the fish tank
And behind a chair
And under the bed
'Where are you going?'
Back into the starry night
House to house has no fright.
'Goodbye bunny.'

Bradley Witt (8)
Hill View Primary School

GHOST

Coal black eyes
Body as white as a sheet
Ghostly music
Haunting houses
Your hideous face
Your wicked smile
And of course the occasional
Sound of *Aaaarrrggghhh!*

Tom Johnson (8)
Hill View Primary School

A DOG'S LIFE

A bit too big
A little too small
Too fuzzy for me
Too fat to crawl.

Before you hold it tight
And lift it in the car
Remember its appetite
It'll eat more than you by far.

Let's just see
Which pup is best
For him or her and, of course, *me!*

Jessica Rabbetts (9)
Hill View Primary School

THE PLANET SMOG

When I landed on the Planet Smog,
The inhabitants looked like dogs!
Four-legged and fluffy and were playing
With a big green log.
They were leaping and bounding, pouncing and
Springing all over the foggy planet!
I was surprised and bewildered by the
Swirling, grey smog clouding around my face.
Alas it was boggy, it smelled very doggy,
And I'll never return to that place!

Charlotte Spenceley (9)
Hill View Primary School

UNIVERSE

Stars, stars everywhere,
Planets, planets everywhere.
Nine planets I can see
Mercury
Venus
Earth
Mars
Jupiter
Saturn.
I can see
Uranus
Pluto
Neptune. Can you see
Comets, comets everywhere? Speeding.
Comets a blur!
Our universe.

Leigh Stanger (9)
Hill View Primary School

SNOWY WINTER

Heavy snow
Slushy ice
Slippery roads
Snowball fights
Chilly houses
Snowy grass
Red faces
Hands numb.

Robert Williams (9)
Hill View Primary School

KANGAROOS

Kangaroos can jump as high as the moon
I hope they come back very soon
Stop dawdling up in the air
And come down here you naughty pair.

Down here I glance up above
Nothing but a tiny dove
I look up again in the air
I hope you are somewhere.

I hear a sound and look above
I see again the little dove
And down the path I see you
You're my friend the kangaroo!

Rebecca Love (9)
Hill View Primary School

COSMIC SPACE

Up and up I go.
What can I see up there?
It's very dark and very cold.
Don't you think?

A green thing.
What is it?
An alien maybe.
Help! It's got me!
SOS to planet Mars.

Kayley Milton (9)
Hill View Primary School

TRAVELLING THROUGH SPACE

I am a speck of light,
Come travelling with me on my flight.
I am travelling through space,
I'm going to see Mercury's face.

Wow, I just shot past Venus, it's hot!
The hottest planet of the lot.
Then there's Earth, lovely water, very clear,
Somewhere there, there's Blackpool pier.

Oh look, there's Mars, it's very red,
I feel like going back to bed.
There's Jupiter with a big red spot,
From far away it looks like a tiny dot.

Saturn with its rings,
Has lots of different things.
Oh Uranus, it is really green,
Look through a telescope and it can be seen.

Neptune and its colour blue,
Come and see it, please, please do.
Oh look there's Pluto, the end of the line,
Now I've finished I feel fine.

Sabrina Booth (9)
Hill View Primary School

THE SPACE RACE

There was once a space race between America and Russia
They tried to get people on the moon
faster than an erupting gusher,
Then the Americans got some people into space,
And Neil Armstrong became the first man
on the moon and won the space race.

Buzz Aldrin was the second man on the moon,
He got there just as soon,
As Neil Armstrong 29 years ago,
I bet NASA as they left Earth thought *uh oh!*
But they didn't need to,
All the astronauts needed to worry about was getting home
and eating that food that tasted like goo.

Dean Pullen (9)
Hill View Primary School

BONFIRE

Roasting hot
Burning
Sparks flicker in the air
Slowly rising then gigantic
Drifting at the top.

Spitting quickly
A colour like orange makes me hot.

Rebekka Jordan (8)
Hill View Primary School

FOOTBALL

The whistle has blown
It's kick-off all right!
People shooting, passing, scoring . . .
Crowds are shouting, urging the players on
'Foul!' the referee calls.
I don't know how
He kicks it over the goalie's head.
The crowd are delighted
One nil to us, the end is near.
People are leaving, all in a rush!
Now it's the end and I must go!

Lee Buxton (9)
Hill View Primary School

BLAST-OFF

5, 4, 3, 2, 1, Blast off.
I was launched into space,
The earth was shrinking
at a phenomenal pace.
My food was floating away,
it looked like a chase,
Out I went into space.

I put on my spacesuit
and went out of the door,
No I'll just go back
and get some more.

James Hillier (9)
Hill View Primary School

WHY DOES IT HAVE TO RAIN TODAY?

I'm bored stiff. I want to play.
Why does it have to rain today?
Look out of the window. It's pouring down with rain!
It's splashing on the window-pane!

I can't do anything because my mum's gone out . . .
All I want to do is shout!
Look the sun's come out, *Wow! Hooray!*
Now I can go out to play.

At last some sun.
Oh what fun!
Now I've got homework to do . . .
I hate homework . . . do you?

Amy Rees (9)
Hill View Primary School

VAMPIRES

I went into the castle
And there I saw the vampire.
His red eyes glowing
His fangs smeared with blood.
Spreading his cloak he soared through the sky
He swooped dangerously low.
Then went back into the sky
Screeching in a high pitched voice
Quickly tiptoed on creaky floors.
I hid behind a cupboard and closed the doors.

Kayley Dancer (9)
Hill View Primary School

NEPTUNE LIFE

Welcome to the planet Neptune,
There're lots of things to do,
The plants are great,
They jump, hop, grow and shrink, all in two seconds.
When you see the animals you'll be surprised.
There're tall ones, short ones, fat ones, thin ones;
The most famous is the zoggle:
He hunts around all night and sleeps all day.
The people think this is all right
So they're sleeping now,
Oh sorry, it's day to the people, let's go.
Bye!

Gemma Finn (9)
Hill View Primary School

THE WEIRDEST BRAIN IN THE UNIVERSE

People call me a weirdo,
Because of my weird brain,
I've thought of telling the teacher,
But the teacher would call me insane.

I haven't been to the doctor,
But I can guess what he would say,
'Go home you stupid brainiac,
Your brain's too weird for me, Doctor Hay.'

Lawrence Wolff (9)
Hill View Primary School

THE PENALTY

'Ow' I've been tripped in the box
The ref points to the spot.
Which way shall I kick it?
Shall I aim it for the left
Or shall I aim it for the right?
The whistle blows, I take a shot
     Goal!
It's in the back of the net
I go wild, the crowd goes bananas
Then I wake up in my pyjamas
I find out that it was all a dream
The very thing that makes me want to
     Scream!

Mark Sinkinson (9)
Hill View Primary School

ICE-CREAM

I like ice-cream
C an I have some more?
E very flavour, more and more.

C oming for more
R ed syrup on top
E very day I have ice-cream
A flake on top
M y milky ice-cream.

Hannah Martin (9)
Hill View Primary School

THE MYSTERY ALIEN

They dwell on a planet not far from the sun.
They come in peace with no one.
Their planet is blue with some green.
They're a bit silly if you know what I mean.
But beneath their soul they're kind and smart
But their planet is falling apart.
The aliens now must be easy to see.
It's you, you, you, and *me!*

Thomas Lockyer (9)
Hill View Primary School

FIREWORK NIGHT

Sizzling stars shooting skywards,
Loud red rockets flickering, flying,
Colourful sparklers spitting smoke
Drifting slowly down to the ground.
Tasty tomatoes shining red
Big bright bangers bursting brightly.

Ryan Clarke (9)
Hill View Primary School

SPACE

In space there is light.
Golden yellow, shining bright.
Lots of planets everywhere
Aliens floating in the air.
The sun is dazzling in the sky
As planets go floating by.

Laura Kimber (9)
Hill View Primary School

I LIKE SCIENCE

First I was afraid I was petrified.
Science is like a bomb going off.
Science is like a drum kit.
And when I had one I was really mad,
Oh no, not I, I will survive
As long as I've got chemistry,
I might just stay alive!

Siân Tilly (9)
Hill View Primary School

THE STORM

Lightning flashing across the sky
Thunder banging like a drum
Rain falling down to Earth
Wind whistling through the trees.
Tornadoes wrecking buildings
Boats sinking in the sea
Drowning people clinging to rocks.

Daniel Martin (9)
Hill View Primary School

THE LITTLE RED SAUCER

When I visited the moon it was totally bare
There wasn't a speck of dust in sight, nor a little pear
Then suddenly up above me hovered a little red saucer,
(Like the one Mum got from Aunt Agernorer)
And inside was a little green alien, who suddenly coughed;
And the saucer flew off.

Rainbow Wilcox (9)
Hill View Primary School

LIGHT

I was nothing
Then I was light
I shine ever so bright
I burn with flames
And gases too
So don't look at me
I'm ever so bright
And burning too with light.

Dean Hillier (9)
Hill View Primary School

PENGUINS

Funny little men
Dressed in dinner suits
Jumping from rock to rock
Darting through waves
Catching fish all day
Snap! There goes another one.

Cherith Webb (9)
Hill View Primary School

SPACE

High up in the sky
All the planets shine and glow like the stars,
Some asteroids like stars come down from nowhere,
Burn like the sun,
And people look up high and see them glowing,
Shining from nowhere.

Sarah Gardner (9)
Hill View Primary School

THE BIG BANG

Is it a balloon bursting?
Or a missile exploding?
It could be vibrating the Earth right now!
Is it a big collision
It might be the solution
With a deafening bang
Plus a frightening sound
But I could be dreaming about the bang.

Laurence Upshon (9)
Hill View Primary School

ALIENS

Aliens are mean
Aliens are cool
But not the one at our school
He plays and plays all day long
He sometimes gets his fractions wrong.

Sam Firmin (9)
Hill View Primary School

SPACE

Twirling, twirling round the sun,
They all go round, one by one.
Some are big, and some are small
But Venus is the brightest of all.
Jupiter with the red spot, the biggest of them all.

Louise Light (9)
Hill View Primary School

WHITE

What is white? I know white,
White is the colour of the fluffy clouds.
What is white? I know white,
White is the colour of the planes in the sky.

What else can be white?
A feathery swan is white,
A graceful dove is white,
And the flower petals of daisies are white.

What else can be white?
Drawing paper can be white,
Warm socks can be white,
And squeaky chalk can be white.

What else can be white?
Maybe you can think of some more,
Like the horsehair bow for a violin,
And the fate of a ghost,
In the darkness of the scary sing . . .
White!

Leoni Kurt (9)
King's Park Primary School

ROCKET, ROCKET

Rocket, rocket flies to the moon
Fast as it can
Then rocket, rocket flies back to Earth
With people on it.

Jamie Miller (8)
King's Park Primary School

My Bedroom

I must keep my bedroom tidy
My mother always said
But it is not easy
As I chuck things off my bed!

My cuddly toys, paper and all
Often under my bed.
And where did my socks go to
So I can go to school?

Yesterday I lost my pen
But found some mouldy bread
Perhaps it's time to start keeping my room tidy
As my mother said.

Charlie Smith (8)
King's Park Primary School

Teachers' Secrets

I would love to know
What teachers do.
Do they play or do they sew?
Do they watch TV all day
Or do they cook dinner on a tray?
Do they hang their clothes up
Or do they let them drip in a cup?
The secrets will last for ever and ever
We will find out if we work together.
But all I know is different teachers have different secrets!

Chloe Helen Palmer (9)
King's Park Primary School

SCHOOL DAY

Nine o'clock it's time for school,
Mr Biddle's on the edge,
the wind just started singing,
on the window ledge.

Come on to assembly,
time to praise the Lord,
come back for some English,
written on the board.

We come back from play,
to a great big sum,
we're all losing patience,
waiting for lunch to come.

Now it's time for science,
why can't we do something good,
all the other pupils
agree, and think we should.

Again we come in from playtime,
this time it is art,
Mr Biddle's drawing,
a pony with a cart.

Hey! Look at the clock,
the time is half past three,
now the clock is at this time,
we can go, *yippee!*

Jonathan Sims (9)
King's Park Primary School

BLACK

Black is a blackbird that sits in my garden
Black is the cat that sits up my tree
Black is the darkness that comes every night
Black is a witch that sits on a broomstick
Black is the cloud before it rains
Black is the ending of fun and games
Black is the bat that flies in the night
Black is a limousine in the shop window
Black is the lead that is in my pencil
Black is when you have a cut or when you
hurt yourself
Black is the squishy mud that is in my garden
Black is the dust that is on my grandfather clock.

Jon Tamagna (9)
King's Park Primary School

BLACK

Black is the bat that flies round your bed
The stallion galloping in the wind
Black is the sad colour of a funeral that reminds
me of death
Black is the colour of the midnight sky in the
pitch dark night
When I hear the word black
a flashing line shoots down my back
Black is a beetle stumbling through the mud
finding its way home
These are some of the things that are black
Can you think of some more?

Laura Palmer (9)
King's Park Primary School

RED

Red is the colour of boiling hot fire that
heats the house
Red is the colour of a bright rose in the
wind
Red is the colour of blood
Red is the colour of the bright sunset
in the sky
Red is a post box in the street
Red is the colour of sports cars
Red is the colour of my rubber and my
lips
Red is the colour of my teacher's
chair and a fire burning
Red is the colour of my troll's hair
Red is the colour of a pretty dress
Red is the colour of a tomato
in my sandwich.

Jemeila Tourh (9)
King's Park Primary School

GREEN

Green is the dewy grass in the everlasting countryside,
Green is seaweed glistening in the seashore sun,
Green is a gooseberry, hairy and sour,
Green is the lettuce you put in salad,
Green is the stalk of an opening flower,
Green is the turf of a football pitch,
Green is ivy creeping up walls.

Robert Donnelly (9)
King's Park Primary School

BLUE

Blue is the cloudless sky
Blue is the blue bird flying up high
Blue is the sparkling swimming pool
Blue is the sweatshirt I wear to school
Blue are the heatwaves that crawl along the
ground without a sound
Blue are my clear blue eyes that match my
fair hair
Blue is my profile with all my work in
Blue is a soft light feather falling to the ground
Blue is the shiver running up and down my spine
Blue . . .

Megan Harling (9)
King's Park Primary School

MY BABY BROTHER

My baby brother he sits and sucks his thumb,
Then he shouts and screams because he wants his mum.
My baby brother when I hold him he is happy
Except when he has a leaky nappy.
My mum tucks him into bed
As he lays down his little head
In the morning he needs to have a feed
Before I go to school I hold him tight
And give him a hug and tell him I'll see him tonight.

Megan Baker (8)
King's Park Primary School

LATE!

S chool is soon approaching,
C oat, gloves, hat and shoes,
H elp my flask is leaking,
O h no! There's knots in my shoes,
O h help I've missed the bus!
L ate in comes the teacher late, late in comes the class,
    I suppose I'm not the only one with a leaking flask!

Emma Balderstone (8)
King's Park Primary School

FLYING

If I could fly I would fly in a tree
And watch the people below me
Then I would fly high in the sky
Way up where the white clouds lie
I would sit on a cloud with a bird's eye view
I would like to fly would you?

Daniel Benham (8)
King's Park Primary School

ROMANCE

The stars remind me of your deep blue eyes.
Your lips are as red as the red, red rose.
Your hand is the softest thing on Earth.
Your voice is as quiet as the wind.

Jessica Fletcher (9)
King's Park Primary School

OUR TEACHER

In class 4AB our teacher is great,
he never ever makes us late.
I think the thing that makes him mad,
is when we children are being bad.
Or when Dania makes Farah laugh,
or when we're looking at Spice Girls photographs.
In class 4AB our teacher is great,
he never ever makes us late.
He's got a great selection of ties,
and he never, ever, ever lies.

Carla Miles (9)
King's Park Primary School

CHOCOLATE

Chocolate all different makes,
I love the smell of chocolate cakes.
Yummy chocolate sensation,
It's the favourite of the nation.

Galaxy Swirls all wrapped in gold,
Let's go out shopping I hope they're
not all sold.
Easter eggs, chocolate money,
What about a bouncing bunny.

Gooey, creamy, lovely and dreamy,
In my purse my fingers are fumbling,
Oh dear listen to my tummy rumbling.

Kate Kellaway-Moore (9)
Milldown Middle School

TRUE BLUE

True blue the colour true blue,
Lord gave us the colour true blue.

We use it for all kinds of things
Like that blue covered book you never read
Your blue coated duvet you never need.

That blue water in the sea
Your mum's picture of a pink and blue tree.

True blue the colour true blue
Lord gave us the colour true blue.

That little blue Power Ranger
That really small bear in danger.

Being bored to death in assembly,
Being freezing cold in the middle of the sea.

That mouldy home-made bread nobody ever eats
Feeling dead after eating 1,000 treats.

True blue the colour true blue,
Lord gave us the colour true blue.

Kim Fendley (9)
Milldown Middle School

THE NOISE

What's that noise?
Is it a monster coming to eat me,
Is it a very very scary zombie
Or is it an owl or something boring?
No it's just my brother snoring!

Simon Hayter (9)
Milldown Middle School

WEATHER

First of all it's just rainy,
then it starts to get really windy,
then hail starts to come,
tapping on the window,
getting louder . . . louder.
I thought it was going to snow
but it didn't unfortunately.
Then everything starts to go,
first the hail goes,
then the wind,
then shortly after the rain goes,
and everything is calm.

Sarah Morris (9)
Milldown Middle School

BLUE

Blue is the colour of the sea
Blue is the colour of water
Blue is the colour of bluebirds
Blue is the colour of bluebells
Blue is the colour of blueberries

Blue is a cold colour
But it's quite bright and light
Or it can be dark
Blue is my favourite colour
Even though it can be quite sad at times!

Ben Wentworth (9)
Milldown Middle School

FRIDAY THE THIRTEENTH

It's Friday the thirteenth
and something is bound to go wrong
I've been waiting for something
to happen all day long.
It's now 3 o'clock
and school has been fine
until I am standing in the bus line.

While waiting for the bus
there was a bit of a fuss.
The bus had crashed
and the windscreen has smashed.
Mrs Burge had a moan
'How am I going to get them home?'
Mum was waiting at the gate
she shouted 'Why are you late?'

'It's Friday the thirteenth!' I said.

Rebecca Whalley (9)
Milldown Middle School

FOOTBALL CLUB

Football club is great
Thursdays I can't wait
I kick the ball
Then I fall
Jump up quick
Pass to Nick
Get a goal that's great
Dirty knees covered in mud
I really like football club.

Gavin Kerby (9)
Milldown Middle School

COLOURS

Yellow is hot,
Fire is very very hot,
Yellow is the colour of the
Burning hot sun,
Yellow is the colour of the
Slithery sand.

Orange is the colour of the
Really hot burning sun,
Orange is the colour of the
Really hot fire,
Orange is a really hot colour.

Blue is the colour of
The sky,
Blue is the colour of
The deep blue sea,
Blue is a boy colour,
Blue is a really sad colour.

You can mix different colours.

Charlotte Adams (9)
Milldown Middle School

THE COLOUR YELLOW

Yellow is the glowing sun glowing bright as gold,
Yellow is Laa-Laa the Teletubby,
Yellow is really fun!
Sand is yellow too, the same as yellow paint
Daffodils glow like trumpets, yellow is like
a duck's beak that makes a loud annoying noise.

Ringing bells ringing away
Pencil cases in the class with funny yellow
faces on.
Yellow feels like lemon juice going down my
throat.
Yellow is a great big fire lighting all around
Yellow makes me feel really good and enjoy
myself.

Anthony Woodruff (9)
Milldown Middle School

THE THIRD WORLD

Sad tears
trickling down your face
you only live in a cardboard box
you have no better place.
Searching through bins
just to find a bit of food
only to find nothing more than a tin of
mouldy apples that hadn't been stewed.
You beg for money without any luck
people just leave you there,
while rubbish flies off a truck.
Dust blows past and chewing gum
sticks to your feet
if only the world were a better place
then everyone could sit by the fire
and warm their cold feet
and be fed fairly, not to live on the
cold dusty street.

Rebecca Hunterwood (9)
Milldown Middle School

COLOURS

What is pink?
Pink is the colour of candyfloss at the fair.

What is red?
Red is the colour of a rose and the sun and when
I am mad.

What is blue?
Blue is the colour of the sea and it makes me
happy.

What is white?
White is bright white paint, shiny and new.

What is yellow?
Yellow is the bright summer sun.

What is green?
Green is the tall oak tree reaching up to the sky.

Philip Martin (9)
Milldown Middle School

COLOURS OF SUMMER

Summer is here bring up a cheer,
Yellow sunflowers have sprouted out of the green grass
Blue eyes looking at a blue sky early in the morning
In summer it is a time to play under the hot yellow sun
Red fox is here in its golden brown coat
Children are playing in their summer dresses
Dogs playing in their black and white coats
People playing quick cricket in the snow.

Tanya Pentney (9)
Milldown Middle School

COLOURS OF SPRING

Purple flowers, rainbow showers,
Indigo rainbow,
Nice blue sky, birds flying by,
Knight dressed in black, holding a sack.

Yellow for the sun, I am having fun,
Eight yellow plates, on three yellow gates,
Light green leaves, on the trees.
Loud red, is it the colour of your head,
Orange chalk, let's have a long walk,
White clouds floating by, what a bright blue sky.

Bright yellow, I said hello,
Lucky you, what bright blue shoes.
Unlike you, I like your yellow shoe,
Evening skies, open your eyes.

Naomi Kendrick (9)
Milldown Middle School

THE COLOUR ORANGE

Orange is the sunlight and bright
Orange is lava from steaming hot volcanoes.
Traffic lights and big bites of big fat
Juicy orange flavoured sweets.
Orange pens and feathers of hens
Orange chalk and broad pencil cases
All these things and others too
Orange makes me joyful and hot like
I'm in a pot with the sun.

Glen Wareham (9)
Milldown Middle School

CRAZY COLOURS

Pink is for flowers
Ice-cream is pink
Noses are pink when they are warm
Knitting wool is pink.
Blue is the sky
Light can be blue
Under you there are waves
Exit signs are blue and so are you.
Black as night
Lights are off
Adults are scared
Children cry
Kids hide under the blankets.

Stacey White (9)
Milldown Middle School

COLOUR

Red is for blood
Green is for unripe bananas
Yellow is for sun
Blue is for sky
Orange is for tangerines
Purple is for lavender
White is for a ghost
Black is for badness
Gold is for treasure
Silver is for fools' gold
Bronze is for statues
Brown is for dirt
Navy is for the Royal Navy.

Luke Mason (9)
Milldown Middle School

Colour Yellow

I drink my yellow lemonade with a slice of lemon to suck
in front of the bright yellow sun.
As I sit there feeling happy I watch the yellow flowers
flowing in the wind.
I lay back in the lovely yellow deck chair and watch the
little kittens play with the long yellow ribbons.
Then I sit down on my yellow mat and polish my little
pretty shells.
Soon it starts to get a little dark so I suck my round yellow
lolly.
Then the stars come out that twinkle and shine.
Then the moon comes out, a full moon it is and then the
peaceful sound of the garden sends me to sleep with a
wonderful glazing glow on my face.

Holly Morrison (9)
Milldown Middle School

The Colour Yellow

Yellow is a pretty colour that is bright like flashes of lightning.
The sun is yellow like banana milkshake, sugar paper and
blobs of yellow paint.
Yellow makes me excited, happy like a summer holiday.
Yellow is lots of elastic bands that can stretch as far as
they want to go.
Yellow is Liverpool's away top as they play football.
Sometimes yellow is the colour of a wasteland with
lots of rubbish around.

Christopher Wareham (9)
Milldown Middle School

COLOURS

What is pink?
>Pink is candyfloss , a squealing pig.

What is red?
>Red is roses, poppies too.

What is blue?
>Blue is icy water, water to swim in.

What is white?
>White is bright like a light.

What is yellow?
>My box is yellow like the sun in the sky.

What is green?
>Trees are green the same as grass.

Lisa Plested (9)
Milldown Middle School

THE COLOUR YELLOW

Yellow is a baby chick just hatched,
and also a banana milkshake that is thick and creamy.
Yellow is sand on the beach,
yellow makes me happy.
Yellow is the colour of my budgie,
also the colour of a tiger ready to pounce.
Yellow makes me jolly,
and also joyful.
Yellow is the colour of a slithery snake,
it is the colour of the Simpsons on TV.
Yellow is the sun way up there,
yellow makes me excited.

Thomas Hill (9)
Milldown Middle School

THE COLOUR BLUE

Blue is the rainbow blue is in the sky.
When I see blue it makes me think about
dolphins and blue whales in the ocean blue.
Every time I look out of my window I see
blue blue blue. You can get blue T-shirts
in the blue shops along the blue waves of
the sea.
But when I look out of my window, I don't
always see the sky but the violets also.
I love the colour blue.
I wear a blue tie, blue shirt, just blue blue blue.
Blue makes me feel cold and frozen like I'm in
the ocean blue, all frozen and cold.

Tara Cheese (9)
Milldown Middle School

GREEN

Green is some grapes,
Green is the country,
Green is a pretty colour,
Green is the fresh air of freedom.
Green are the plants swaying in the breeze,
Green is seaweed, crabs hiding there,
Green is an enjoyable colour and nice and warm.
Green you can eat nice fresh food,
Green is spring,
Green is a colour,
Green is a Christmas tree with a fairy on top,
Green is a colour.

Candice Asher (9)
Milldown Middle School

WHY COLOURS?

Green fields but why green what does it mean?
Red but what does it mean,
angry, happy or mad?
Dark blue is it now, is it moody, boring or glum?
Light blue why is the sky light blue?
Purple but why purple pansies when what are
mansies?
Yellow but why a yellow sun when we can have
a pink sun?

Jessica Toledo (9)
Milldown Middle School

THERE'S A MOUSE IN THE HOUSE

Squeaking in the night,
Got a lot of fright,
Ahh there's a mouse in the house
He is about to pounce on the table,
If he's able,
Ahh there's a mouse in the house
He likes pinching food,
He is very, very rude,
Ahh there's a mouse in the house,
He's got a thin short tail
I wish he would go to jail
But then I'd be bored
Ahh there's a mouse in the house.

Eleanor Hunt & Briony Warren (7)
Radipole CP School

MY SOCK PUPPET

My sock puppet's friendly
funny too
Blue eyed and hasn't
got much to do.

He's shy in the day
and rude in the night
He needs to learn his left and right,
keep an eye open he might take a bite!

He's got a wobbly tooth
oops it's out.
Hey you over there,
get a tissue otherwise I'll shout!

Hannah Gibson (7)
Radipole CP School

MY SOCK PUPPET

My sock puppet is a mouse
He has got his own little house
And he has got his own little bed
But he often sleeps on the floor
I love my little mouse
Whose name is Floppy
But he is very sloppy.

Amelia Williams (7)
Radipole CP School

WHAT A BUSY TIME!

L ondon's dockland light railway
O ver the school playground
N ight-time busy, cars all around
D own the River Thames, people living on boats
O ff went trains, clash, clash, clash
N earby people scurry along, dash, dash, dash!

Shirley Dorran (9)
St Mary's School, Beaminster

LONDON NOISES

L ashing River Thames
O range cranes, mad traffic
N ight-time noises, crash! Crash! Crash!
D ocklands light railway roaring over the school
O h I don't have a clue what to do
N ow here comes the underground train *Argh!*

Natalie Stewart (9)
St Mary's School, Beaminster

THE JOKER

Crick crack break my back
shuffle the cards in the pack
I'll make your queen sticky and
king too
I'll even glue your ace to your jack
because I'm the joker in the pack.

Michael Livens (9)
St Mary's School, Beaminster

LONDON

People starving
some sleep rough
rich people rushing
Tony Blair now in a huff

Cold children crying
can't sleep at night
Big Ben booming
at such a height

Beggars begging
all they can do
trains rumbling
as they pass through.

Nick Hill (9)
St Mary's School, Beaminster

SPACE

There was a girl called Janet
Who visited a planet
It was very far
For she visited Mars

A moon man she met
Janet said I love this planet
Then back in the car
With Ma and Pa she drove very far.

Tia Corry Wright (7)
St Mary's School, Beaminster

DREAMS OF SPACE AND TEAMS

Everyone needs space
A beautiful place
I had a dream
Of a beautiful stream
I need lots of space
I want the perfect place
I just bet
That I will get
A perfect score for my team
That would be a lovely dream
I need to find
Some space.

Laura Crabb (8)
St Mary's School, Beaminster

HOLIDAY

The girls
Who lay in the sun
Are reading their books
The men are catching the fish in their nets
People twirl
My ice-cream is melting
Beautiful pearls
I am having fun
I saw a book
I sat on my mat
People whirl.

Lydia Olsen (7)
St Mary's School, Beaminster

UNDER THE SEA

As the waves
Whoosh at the seaweed
Starfish slither along
The golden slippery sand.
Crabs scuttle along the rocks.
Fish swirl, swish
Their tails in and out
Cracks between
The old ships
From long ago.
Days pass
Nights grow longer.
As winter comes
Crabs scuttle
In cracks.
Fish swirl
To find shelter.

Hannah Clark (8)
St Nicholas & St Lawrence School

SPACE

Space is dark
Space is full of planets
Space is full of rocks
Space is full of asteroids
It is dark as dark can be
Meteorites shoot across the sky
The stars make constellations
The planets are growing
Aliens everywhere.

Robert West (9)
St Thomas Garnet's Primary School

THE SUN

The sun is fat
It sat and sat
Getting very fat!
It still sat and sat
Till it was completely fat
And it prayed to the Lord above.
There was a man called Dearth
Who thought that the earth was flat.
He never went sailing anywhere
For he thought
When you got to the edge
You fell upon the sun
You would burn to death
And die!

Sean Dingley (8)
St Thomas Garnet's Primary School

MY TEDDY BEAR

My teddy bear
Hasn't much hair

He sits on my bed
And lays on his head
My teddy bear sits there and stares
Watching all the others eat their juicy pears

He wears a bow tie
And eats apple pie

My teddy bear
Hasn't much hair.

Rebecca Green (9)
St Thomas Garnet's Primary School

COSMIC

The glowing colours of space
Remind me of a very big place
The darkness is very scary
And bangs are out there rarely.

I went in a rocket up there
And there were rockets flying everywhere
The planets are Jupiter and Mars
And I saw lots and lots of stars.

The sun is very very bright
That it gave me such a fright
And if we went too near it
We would burn every little bit.

Anne Henman (8)
St Thomas Garnet's Primary School

COSMIC

Space is like a pitch black room
With little lights on as stars
And with planets all around you
And it would be very hot.

There would be very big shooting stars
But they are very rare
And the sun would be very bright.

You would see flying saucers
And spaceships and rockets
On the way you would see different galaxies
And planets.

Ben Hitchcock (9)
St Thomas Garnet's Primary School

GETTING HOME

As I walked home in the rain
I got lost and fell down a drain
On to a very big rat
Sitting on a red mat.

I asked him to show me out
He said over there - no doubt!
I climbed out in a minute and a half
Still hearing his horrible ratty laugh.

Round the corner there was a lovely sight
My green front door on the right
I was glad to be safely home
In my house with my gnomes.

Elizabeth McMahon (7)
St Thomas Garnet's Primary School

ANOTHER DAY

Boys shout, girls giggle,
All silence, pencils squiggle,
Bell goes, everyone knows,
A boring day today.

Boys kick, girls flee,
Everyone knows it's time for tea,
Bell goes, line up,
John says 'Shut up!'

Go home, jump with glee,
Mum's got some chips for tea.
Sit down with a full belly,
Let's all watch some telly!

Kae Drinkwater (8)
St Thomas Garnet's Primary School

MR BUMP

Mr Bump likes to jump
High into the air.
When he lands he hits his head
Banging it on a chair.

Up he gets and rubs his head,
But as it's cut and bleeding,
The doctor comes and stitches it up
And says it will soon be healing.

Days go by and his head gets better
And he's feeling fine.
But Mr Bump who likes to jump,
Soon repeats this rhyme.

James Ingram-Johnson (9)
St Thomas Garnet's Primary School

ALIENS AND SPACEMEN

Spacemen coming here and there
Aliens attacking spacemen
Aliens blowing up earth
More spacemen coming
More spacemen blowing up too!
Stars falling
The world coming to an end
Aliens' plan working!
The world falling
Aliens win!

Lee Fordham (8)
St Thomas Garnet's Primary School

THE SEASONS

In spring, the birds sing at dawn and build nests.
The bulbs pop up and the trees blossom.
I love spring.

In summer I like to go to the beach.
It is nice and hot.
I like to eat ice-creams.
I love summer.

In autumn the leaves turn brown, red, yellow and gold.
The squirrels collect nuts and animals hibernate.
I love autumn.

In winter it is cold and chilly.
I wear ear muffs, gloves and a scarf.
I like to put the carrot on the snowman.
I love winter.

Christopher Linda (8)
St Thomas Garnet's Primary School

SPACE

Space is dark, big and quiet,
its creepy comets come up behind you and
miss you by an inch.
You take a peek to see space
then a flying saucer comes up and you faint.
You've seen the galaxy, you've seen earth,
seen the craters, stars, solar system, space station
all in one universe.

Sean Atkinson (8)
St Thomas Garnet's Primary School

The Beginning Of Space

The *big bang* started if off,
It made the huge universe.
Galaxies soon formed,
With billions of stars,
But black holes came,
And started twirling.
Then the solar system appeared,
With the sun.
Soon after the sun flung out planets,
And rocks like comets,
More rocks fell off planets,
Called moons,
And that's how space began.

Christopher Short (9)
St Thomas Garnet's Primary School

My Guinea Pig

My guinea pig is sweet
And she likes to eat.
Her name is Coca
And she likes to sleep

Her fur is black and ginger
And she likes to nibble my finger.
I like to bring her into play
But at night-time she has to go away.

Theresa Gillings (7)
St Thomas Garnet's Primary School

HAPPINESS

Happiness is when I can ride my bike
Happiness is when I can go out at night
Happiness is when you can go out to play
Happiness is when it has been the funniest day
Happiness is when I can stay up very late
Happiness is when I can sleep in after eight
Happiness is when there's no work to do
Happiness is when Mum does things for you.

Paul Malin (10)
St Thomas Garnet's Primary School

COOKING

When I cook
I use a book.
When I smell smoke
I start to choke.
When I see steam
I start to scream.
When I see meat
I run with my feet.

Anna Wazejewski (7)
St Thomas Garnet's Primary School

JUST ME

I know sometimes I'm happy
I know sometimes I'm glad
I know sometimes I'm silly
I know sometimes I'm sad

Sometimes I like to work
Sometimes I like to play
Sometimes I like to stop and think
Sometimes I like to pray

Sometimes I like to help
Sometimes I like to leap
Sometimes I like to run and jump
Sometimes I like to sleep

Of course I'm never naughty
Of course I'm never mad
Of course I'm never greedy
Of course I'm never bad

I know I'm not an angel
I know I'm not a saint
I know I'm not *quite* perfect
If I was my mum would faint.

Emma Tuck (9)
St Thomas Garnet's Primary School

MAGIC

You have a hat out of which you pull a hare,
Look out, look out,
Magic is everywhere.

A light match becomes a rose,
Snap your fingers,
Watch everyone doze.

Spin around and disappear,
No, no, no,
I'm over here.

Ping, boom, boof, poof!
All magicians must stay aloof,
Or all their secrets might as well be . . .
Mushed up pea!

Some are great,
Some aren't at all,
I'm talking about tricks,
Large and small.

It's magic!
Magic!
Magic!

Gareth Wilson (9)
St Thomas Garnet's Primary School

ONE SUNNY SUNDAY MORNING

One sunny Sunday morning,
When things were getting rather boring
Just then . . .
I saw a flying pen.

This pen flew a bit more
And said, 'What do you take me for?
I'm really getting rather bored,
I've had enough of this fraud.'

The pen pointed to a rubber
'I've had it with his childish blubber!
All he does is complain,
He should be in great shame.'

Just then the rubber said,
'It's because I don't get fed.
He took away my chewy-chew
And all I said was, 'Boo-hoo!'

'He's always saying 'boo-hoo'
And that is really true.
I had to take away his food,
And now I'm in a real mood.'

Then I really drew the line,
'Rubber how dare you whine,
Pen get out of your mood
And give him back his food.'

Then from that day,
Happen what may,
They were the best of friends
And that's how the story ends.

Alexander Simmons (9)
St Thomas Garnet's Primary School

HAPPINESS IS

Slumber parties,
Seeing relations,
Giving people presents,
When people get married,
Going shopping,
Having no homework,
Happiness is lots of things.

Fionnuala Craven (9)
St Thomas Garnet's Primary School

SPACE STATION

The rocks, comets and fireballs,
The sun, the moon and shooting stars,
Are all in space.
There are planets all colourful and glowing,
And they can all be seen through a telescope.
There is no gravity in space,
But there are spaceships and aliens, but no air.

Oisin O'Leary (8)
St Thomas Garnet's Primary School

SUMMER

Birds fly in the sky
The cats play all through the day
Lots of frogs sit on logs.
All the mice eat lots of rice.
And I sit in the sun
And have some fun.

Bethany Wildeman (7)
St Thomas Garnet's Primary School

DILOLLIDOT

I have a little friend
Who is very very strange
He won't eat anything
Or drink anything
So I decided to take him
Back to the moon.
His little cottage is called
A cute little name
Zlollipop Cottage.
My little friend's name
Is Dilollidot.
The little alien said
Everyone on your planet
Said the moon was made
Of cheese.
But he said it was made of
Milky Way.
My little friend here
Looks a bit like an orange
He has a few freckles
But not many.
So that's the end
Of my friend Dilollidot
I left him there on the moon
For the rest of his life.

Anya Browne (9)
St Thomas Garnet's Primary School

THE WEATHER

The sun is hot in summer,
We go down to the beach.
It warms you up,
It makes you smile.
But summer only lasts a while.

Then autumn comes
Then thunder and lightning,
To zap the house,
The rain soaks the trees,
This is the season when the storms come.

Winter's coming, now's the day.
The snow falls silently, thick and fast,
Snowmen built,
Let's have snowball fights,
Santa's on his way.

Here is spring,
When April showers,
Fall softly on the lovely flowers,
Bluebells, tulips and daffodils,
With bright green leaves say a big Thank You.

Oh Lord you are so clever - so many different kinds of weather.

Grace Watt (8)
St Thomas Garnet's Primary School

THE UNIVERSE

The sun is hot
The moon is cold
The sky is filled with stars,
The planets sing a song of joy
Among the sun and stars.

Then the moon came into it
And stopped them having fun,
Which really, really was a shame
For the sun's birthday party,
Was just about to be on.

The moon gave them a punishment
Yes, for the planets, sun and stars,
He actually locked them up for the night
And never ever let them out,
No never let them out.

So that's the end of the universe
No planets, sun or stars,
Just the earth on its own,
And the moon far away.
Or are there a few more?

Laura Sheasby (9)
St Thomas Garnet's Primary School

SUN

I am the sun - don't step on me
I have given you a warning
Dare touch me!
I will scorch you black
Or fry you like a pancake
Don't touch me!
I burn anything that thinks it can pass me
My claws of fire will blaze you down
But on the good side
I give light to everyone, everything
I help flowers to grow
I keep the pouring rain
I am here by day and go by night
In a couple of billion years or so
I will turn off my light
And say goodnight.

James Masson (9)
Sherborne Preparatory School

ASTRONAUT

As I step into my rocket,
I put my hands into my pocket to feel my lucky locket,
I am as scared as a fox,
Fleeing from a hunt.

As I approach the moon,
The grey and cratered moon butterflies
Were flying in my stomach,
I'm scared as a fox,
Fleeing from a hunt! Fleeing from a hunt!

Will we land in the right place,
Having wandered through space?
Bang! We've landed right on the spot,
As I open the hatch
And the sun so hot
Beats down on this barren land.

Will I live here soon?

Sonja Farrell (9)
Sherborne Preparatory School

THE MOON

The moon is a ball of rock,
With craters all shapes and sizes,
It orbits round earth,
Ever since its birth,
With comets crashing,
And meteoroids bashing,
Rotating round and round,
With ice on each pole,
We may be able to live there soon,
Will we pollute the moon?
And burn all its craters,
By launching rockets off its bumpy, lumpy surface,
And throwing rubbish all over its skin,
Driving cars, motorbikes, lorries and vans.
Building factories that belch out smoke,
Will we slowly destroy the moon,
As we are killing earth?

Simon Horner (9)
Sherborne Preparatory School

SATURN

I am Saturn
With an icy ring
My life is happy with Jupiter as king
But when man comes to my land
What will he bring in his hand
Please do not come for you will pollute my planet
Will they build high towers above me?
Will they dig holes inside me?
Will they leave junk around me?
Will they destroy my land?
Will they? Will they? Will they?
I beg them not to come
For I am happy with Jupiter beside me
Please do not change my life.

Mark Corfield-Moore (9)
Sherborne Preparatory School

THE MOON

Up to space,
Through the night sky,
I see stars as I drift by,
I'm off to the moon,
I hope I'm there soon,
I arrive at the moon with a thump and a bump,
Some parts are hot, some parts are cold,
I wonder if there's creatures
I walk on the moon all day,
I see nothing, nothing, nothing,
Is it a place where a man could live,
What has it to give?

Jamie Smibert (8)
Sherborne Preparatory School

Floating Through Space

Planets floating way up high,
Twirling and whirling in the sky,
Astronomers studying stars,
Wondering how to travel to Mars,
Astronauts think they can land on Jupiter
I don't think they can be any stupider.

There are nine planets - some far, some near,
We live on Earth - this planet right here
The giant rings of Saturn,
Look like massive wings,
Pluto is the furthest it looks so dark,
So you couldn't find a place to park.

Venus spits out poisonous gases
So I wouldn't go too near,
Mercury is very queer,
Boiling hot, freezing cold,
Neptune is the king of the sea,
He has prongs as big as could be.

Floating through space,
Planets far and near,
I wonder
Will we ever land here?

Sophie Weller (9)
Sherborne Preparatory School

SPACE

I am a star burning hot,
To you on earth I am just a dot.

I am a comet with a flaming tail,
I'm hot not cold like icy hail.

We are the planets there's nine of us,
We take the same path and don't make a fuss.

We make up the galaxy,
We make up space,
We make up the universe,
All these we embrace.
We might disappear very soon,
Never to be seen again.

Lucy Crocker (8)
Sherborne Preparatory School

THE MOON

Asteroids crashing knocking the Moon
Making craters where aliens might live!
Strange creatures with funny features
Three eyes and ten legs.

Spaceships landing with astronauts leaping out
Racing around in their buggies
Picking up rocks and taking them home.

Now there is ice on the Moon
Should we waste money on this barren satellite
While thousands of people are crying for food
While animals are becoming extinct.

Building rocket launchers on the Moon
To fly to Venus to fly to Mars
To fly round the universe and back
If we do land on the Moon - we'll pollute it very soon.

Robert Smith (9)
Sherborne Preparatory School

THE MOON

The moon is a ball of rock
Small and grey
He lives in space all day.
There's ice on the moon but we've only just found it.
It's on the ground at the north and south pole.
And when we melt it - hip hip hooray
There'll be ice on the moon - but not today.
But what will happen when man comes?
Will they pollute me like Mother Earth?
Will they infect my skin with garbage and smoky fuels?
Will they dig out my organs with drills to end my life?
What if I want them to go away?
Just leave me alone till you know how to keep me alive.

Jonathan Hacking (9)
Sherborne Preparatory School

SPACE

Space is a world of fun
Astronauts come,
Lots of stars burst out high
Up in the light blue sky,
Jupiter has sixteen moons
Or are they really big balloons.
The sun is burning hot
Like a filled up cauldron - a huge pot.

Pluto is the coldest planet
The furthest from the sun,
No one can live there
As it's too cold for everyone,
There's a big green alien
With three eyes,
And two fat thighs
That are rough and cold.

Lucinda James (8)
Sherborne Preparatory School

MARS

Mars is the red planet
It has two moons and an ice cap on top
I want to go to Mars
I want to build a spaceship and land on this mysterious planet
Will there be aliens who can live in the ice?
Will they have polluted their planet like we have on earth?
Who knows! Nobody.

Ratidzo Moyo (9)
Sherborne Preparatory School

CREATURES FROM SPACE

I am the moon,
I travel all day,
Who's that stepping,
All over me?
They're polluting me with garbage,
What can I do? What can I do?
If they only knew!
I am the moon,
I travel all day,
Who's that stamping all over me?
They're polluting my dusty seas,
Stop please! Stop please!
If they only knew.

Jackie Cameron (9)
Sherborne Preparatory School

THE STORM

The rain goes splash on the window
The thunder goes crash, bang,
And frightens little children.

The snow makes a crunching sound,
And plop when it falls on the ground.

Bump, bump, bang, bang,
There goes the thunder again and then.

Snow is coming - snow is gone,
Sun is coming out again.

Lucy Mather (8)
Sticklands VA Primary School

WEATHER POEM

The sunshine shines like a Ruby
but I get sunburnt like a cooked shrimp.
When it rains I splash in puddles,
gurgle, gurgle, gurgle goes the water down the drain.
Squelch, squelch, squelch go my boots down the lane.
Crunch, crunch goes the gravel all the way.

The swosh, swosh of the trees makes me dizzy,
they make my hair blow in my face.
It starts to rain pitter patter, patter pitter,
as the raindrops hit the ground.
We run inside, splat, splat, splat, crush, crush, crush
the rain gets very hard and a storm comes.
Smash, bash, crash : the baby starts to cry
Wah, Wah : the storm stops, so does the rain.

The sun comes up and we go outside and lie in the grass,
baby eats ants but Mum doesn't see.
I lie in the grass and fall asleep.

Molly Davies-Crosby (7)
Sticklands VA Primary School

RAIN

It pitter pats on the window,
It rustles the trees,
It waters the flowers,
And bends the leaves.

The water rushing to the drain,
The clouds return,
And makes more rain,
And pitter pats on the window again.

The rain is good to play in,
Down, down, it falls,
Drip, drip, down the drain,
Next the wind calls

Swoosh, swoosh, the wind blows,
The rain turns to ice,
Swirling, swirling the snow flakes go,
Everything is white and nice.

Jody Mason (8)
Sticklands VA Primary School

RAIN

The sun is setting in the sky.
Rain is very far away.
The sun is fading: we know it's going to rain.

Clouds are coming close until they drop the most.
It rains and rains,
The sun behind the clouds
Trying to get out,
The rain splashes and sprinkles on the ground.

You hear the mumble and the tumble of the rain flooding.
Rain is smashing like broken glass tingling,
Jingling, splashing on the ground,
Rain is rushing down the drain.
Gurgling and rumbling
Tapping on the window like the clip-clop of horses.

Edmond Wright (8)
Sticklands VA Primary School

A Storm

It pings while it sings,
Disappears down drains going glug, glug, glug.
Oh look! It's whizzing and fizzing through the air,
Making sudden hisses, hums, booms and bangs.
Swishing and swaying the trees side to side.
Then a rumble followed by a crash, a flash,
And an occasional *pop!*

I hear a crack then a crash of the trees when they fall to the ground.
Then all the others creak,
And join the first trees on the ground.
Then the rain tips down like a giant bucket of water,
Being thrown down out of the dark grey sky.

Joanne O'Donovan (9)
Sticklands VA Primary School

Weather Poem

Wind is whistling through the air,
Rain is spitting on my hair,
Here comes the rain dripping down,
Splitter, splatter, splitter, splatter.

Leaves, leaves, rustling leaves,
Though it is a sunny day,
Streams are trickling everywhere,
Birds are singing in the air.

Leanne Knight (8)
Sticklands VA Primary School

THE RAIN

Spitter, spatter on the ground,
Splash, splash all around.

Roaring, soaring in a storm,
Swirling, twirling without form.

Bang, bang when it falls,
Bouncing, flouncing like a ball.

Ping - pong on the pane,
Rushing, gushing to the drain.

Ellie Chapman (8)
Sticklands VA Primary School

WEATHER POEM

When I went to post a letter,
The wind blew up my legs,
When I had posted it,
The wind blew me down the road,
Help! Help me!
Good - I am home.
I go to bed, I am scared.
The storm blows the chimney off.
It blows some trees down
But I am safe.

Ashley Jones (7)
Sticklands VA Primary School